English C‹

A TAS___

THE THAMES COUNTRY

and the Chilterns

A Selection of Traditional Local Recipes

STREATLEY REACH

Compiled by
Dorothy Baldock

With paintings by A.R. Quinton
and drawings by Frederick L. Griggs R.A.

SALMON

OLD COTTAGES AT WHITCHURCH

Published by J Salmon Limited,
100 London Road, Sevenoaks, Kent TN13 1BB

Designed by the Salmon Studio
Copyright © 1995 J Salmon Limited
ISBN 1 898435 47 2

Printed in England by J Salmon Limited, Tubs Hill Works, Sevenoaks, Kent

Front Cover: Cottages at Garsington
Back Cover : Marlow from Quarry Woods

Index

THE WITTENHAM CLUMPS

A THAMES BACKWATER

Hollygog Pudding

A farmhouse roly-poly pudding, said to have been first made in the Oxfordshire village of Kiddington.

8 oz. plain flour	4 tablespoons golden syrup, warmed
Pinch of salt	1 teaspoon lemon juice (optional)
4 oz. butter	½ pint milk
3–4 tablespoons water	A little extra butter

Set oven to 400°F or Mark 6. Sift the flour and salt into a bowl, then rub in the butter until the mixture resembles fine breadcrumbs. Add sufficient water to form a stiff dough, then turn out on to a lightly floured surface and roll out into a rectangle between ⅛–¼-inch in thickness. Spread the syrup over the pastry, then sprinkle over the lemon juice, if desired. Roll up like a Swiss Roll, and place in a well buttered ovenproof dish. Pour over sufficient milk to come halfway up the side of the pudding and dot the top with a little extra butter. Bake for 30–40 minutes and serve, cut into slices, with custard or cream. Serves 4–6.

Gammon and Apricot Pie

The combination of gammon, or ham, with apricots dates back at least to Elizabethan days. This recipe is from Buckinghamshire.

4 gammon steaks, approx. 1-inch thick	Black pepper
1–1½ oz. butter	½ oz. sultanas
5 oz. dried apricots, the no-soak type are ideal	¼ pint pork stock
	1–1½ lb. potatoes, peeled and parboiled, then cut into slices

Set oven to 350°F or Mark 4. Fry the gammon lightly on both sides in half the butter. Arrange in a 1½–2-pint pie dish and cover with the apricots. Season lightly with pepper, then sprinkle over the sultanas. Pour on the stock and cover the filling with overlapping layers of potatoes. Melt the remaining butter and brush over the potatoes. Cover the pie with a piece of kitchen foil and bake for 1 hour, then remove the foil and bake for a further 20–30 minutes to brown the potatoes. Serve with carrots and peas. Serves 4.

Berkshire Jugged Steak

A simple, but delicious recipe, that has its origins in the cauldron cookery of the Middle Ages, when a number of different dishes were boiled together in one large pot.

1½–2 lb. rump steak	Salt and black pepper
1 onion, peeled and left whole	1 or 2 teaspoons mushroom
10 cloves	ketchup
2 carrots, peeled and diced	3 sprigs parsley and a small
2 sticks celery, trimmed and	bayleaf, tied together with
diced	a piece of kitchen string

Cut the steak into small, neat cubes and place in a tall narrow casserole that has been rinsed out in cold water. Stick the onion with the cloves and add to the meat. Rinse the carrots and celery in cold water, drain well and add to the meat. Season, then add the mushroom ketchup and *bouquet garni*. Do *not* add any fat, stock or water. Cover the casserole with a piece of kitchen foil and place the lid firmly on top. Place in a saucepan of boiling water, and stew for 2 hours, topping up the water as necessary. Before serving, discard the herbs and the cloves from the onion and then slice the onion and return it to the casserole. Serve with boiled potatoes and a green vegetable. Serves 4–6.

Oxford John

A quickly prepared dish of fresh lamb fried in herbs.

4 lamb steaks approx. 6 oz. each	2 shallots, peeled and very
in weight	finely chopped
1 teaspoon fresh chopped parsley	1 oz. butter
½ teaspoon fresh chopped thyme	½ oz. plain flour
½ teaspoon fresh chopped mint	½ pint lamb stock
Pinch of ground mace	Juice of half a lemon
Salt and black pepper	Croutons

Wipe the lamb steaks with a piece of kitchen paper. Mix together the herbs, spice, seasoning and shallots and coat the lamb steaks lightly with this mixture, pressing down well. Melt the butter in a frying pan and fry the steaks gently, turning occasionally until cooked through. Remove with a slotted spoon and place on a warm serving dish. Stir the flour into the remaining butter in the pan and cook, stirring, for 1 minute, then gradually add the stock and lemon juice. Bring to the boil, stirring, and simmer for 2 minutes. Return the steaks to the pan and simmer for a further 5 minutes. Serve garnished with croutons and accompanied by creamed potatoes and a green vegetable. Serves 4.

Originally Oxford John was made with thick slices of meat cut from a fresh leg of lamb or mutton, but lamb steaks make a delicious substitute.

Eton Mess

*Named after Eton College, this delicious summer dessert
of strawberries, meringues and cream, is also known as Clare
College Mush, after Clare College, Cambridge.*

2 large egg whites	2 lb. fresh strawberries
4 oz. caster sugar	washed, drained well and hulled
1 oz. icing sugar, sifted	3 tablespoons brandy
¾ pint double cream	

Set oven to 250°F or Mark ½. Whisk the egg whites in a clean, grease free bowl, until they are stiff enough not to fall out of the bowl when it is turned upside down. Add half the sugar and whisk in well, then fold in the remaining sugar. Using a tablespoon, drop even piles of the meringue mixture on to a lightly greased baking sheet. Bake for 1½ hours or until the meringues are a soft cream colour with a slightly soft centre. Cool on a wire rack. Reserving a few stawberries for decoration, roughly chop up the remainder, put into a bowl and sprinkle over them the icing sugar and brandy. Chill for 1–2 hours. Whip the cream until it just holds its shape and carefully fold in the strawberries and their liqueur. Crush the meringues and fold into the strawberry mixture. Pile into a glass dish and decorate with the reserved strawberries. Serves 4–6.

If, preferred shop-bought meringues can be used, though home-made ones are undoubtedly nicer in this dessert.

Buckingham Bacon Badger

This boiled pudding is a traditional country way of extending a relatively small amount of meat, and the Buckinghamshire version is always known as a 'badger' because of its well rounded badger-like shape.

1 lb. bacon, de-rinded, and chopped	2 teaspoons chopped fresh sage
1 onion, peeled and finely chopped	Black pepper
1 potato, peeled and finely diced	8 oz. prepared suet crust pastry

Mix together the bacon, onion, potato and sage and season well with pepper. Roll out the pastry on a lightly floured surface to form a rectangle about 12-inches by 9-inches. Spread the bacon mixture over the pastry, leaving about ½-inch around the edges. Dampen the edges, then roll up like a Swiss roll and press the ends together firmly. Wrap up in a clean, well floured pudding cloth and then wrap again in kitchen foil. Tie the ends tightly, but allow the pudding room to expand. Place in a saucepan of boiling water and boil for 2½–3 hours, topping up the water if necessary. Unwrap and serve cut into thick slices, accompanied by thick, brown gravy, boiled potatoes and a green vegetable. Serves 4–6.

If preferred, though it is not traditional, the Badger can be made by lining a greased pudding basin with the pastry, then adding the filling and a pastry lid and steaming for the same length of time.

Windsor Castle Cake

A cake containing ground rice and lemon rind, somewhat on the lines of a Maderia.

4 oz. plain flour	8 oz. caster sugar
½ teaspoon baking powder	Grated rind of a lemon
6 oz. ground rice	2 eggs, beaten
8 oz. butter	½ pint milk
A little sifted icing sugar	

Set oven to 350°F or Mark 4. Sift the flour and baking powder together into a bowl, then add the ground rice. Rub in the butter until the mixture resembles fine breadcrumbs, then stir in the sugar and lemon rind. Add the eggs, combining well, then stir in sufficient milk to produce a soft, dropping consistency. Turn into a well greased and base lined 7-inch round cake tin and bake for 2 hours, until well-risen and golden, covering the top with a piece of kitchen foil of it appears to be browning too quickly. Cool in the tin for 5 minutes, then turn out and place on a wire rack. Before serving, dust the top with a little sifted icing sugar.

WINDSOR CASTLE FROM THE MEADOWS

Rout Biscuits

These sweetmeats were popular accompaniments to a glass of wine or sherry at routs or fashionable gatherings in the 18th and 19th centuries. A Middlesex recipe.

6 oz. caster sugar
6 oz. ground almonds
2 egg whites

A few drops of almond
or ratafia essence
A little beaten egg yolk

Small pieces of glacé cherry, angelica or flaked almond for decoration

Set oven to 350°F or Mark 4. In a bowl, combine the sugar and ground almonds together until evenly coloured. Gradually stir in the egg whites, stirring until the mixture is smooth and firm. Spoon into a piping bag fitted with a small rosette, star or scroll nozzle. Set the biscuits well apart on a greased baking sheet and pipe each one according to inclination. Decorate with a piece of cherry, angelica or flaked almond, brush lightly with beaten egg yolk to give a golden glaze, and bake for 6–7 minutes. Cool on a wire rack.

Aylesbury Game Pie

A rich pie, particularly popular in Victorian and Edwardian times. This version is cooked in a pastry case, but there is another version, still referred to by the same name, that is in fact, a rich game terrine.

1 oz. butter
4 prepared pigeons
1 onion, peeled and chopped
¼ pint beef stock
4 tablespoons sherry
2 oz. salt belly pork
3 oz. fresh white breadcrumbs

8 oz. minced beef or veal
4 tablespoons chopped parsley
Black pepper
Grated rind of half a lemon
1 dessertspoon brandy
12 oz. prepared shortcrust pastry
Beaten egg to glaze

Melt the butter in a saucepan and brown the pigeons all over. Add the onion and cook for 1 minute, then pour over the stock and sherry. Bring to the boil, then cover and simmer for 50 minutes. Remove the pigeons and allow to cool, reserving the stock. Place the pork in a saucepan, cover with cold water, bring to the boil and simmer until tender. Drain and allow to cool, then mince coarsely. Mix together with the breadcrumbs, the pork, the beef or veal, parsley, black pepper, lemon rind and brandy. Then add sufficient stock to bind the mixture. Remove the pigeon meat from the bones. Set oven to 400°F or Mark 6. Roll out the pastry on a lightly floured surface and use two-thirds to line a well greased raised pie mould. Place a layer of pigeon meat on the base, then layer the breadcrumb mixture and pigeon meat alternately, finishing with a layer of breadcrumbs. Cover with the remaining pastry, sealing the edges well and making a steam hole in the centre. Decorate with leaves cut from the pastry trimmings. Brush the top liberally with beaten egg and bake for 1 hour, then lower the oven temperature to 350°F or Mark 4 and bake for a further 30 minutes, covering the top with a piece of kitchen foil if it appears to be browning too quickly. Carefully remove the pie from the mould and brush the sides and top with the remaining beaten egg and return to the oven for a further 10 minutes. Serve hot or cold. Serves 4–6.

Her Majesty's Pudding

A vanilla flavoured custard-cream pudding from Windsor.

1 oz. butter	1 pint milk or single cream
5 eggs	A few drops of vanilla essence
2 oz. caster sugar	A thin strip of lemon peel
	Grated nutmeg

Use ½ oz. butter to grease a 1½ pint ovenproof dish. Beat the eggs and sugar together in a bowl until the sugar has dissolved. Heat the milk or cream in a saucepan with the vanilla essence and lemon peel, until just boiling. Leave to infuse for 30 minutes, then bring back to the boil again. Allow to cool a little, then remove the lemon peel and pour on to the egg mixture, stirring continuously. Strain the mixture into the prepared dish, dot with the remaining butter and sprinkle with nutmeg. Set oven to 325°F or Mark 3. Place the dish in a roasting tin, pour in sufficient boiling water to come halfway up the side of the dish and bake for 35–40 minutes. In order to brown the top, place the pudding on the top shelf of the oven for 2–3 minutes. Serve hot or cold with fresh fruit and accompanied by whipped cream. Serves 4–6.

THE BELL INN, HURLEY

Devilled Mutton

A popular Victorian and Edwardian dish that was often served for breakfast. A Berkshire recipe using lamb, which is now more readily available.

8 slices cold roast lamb, thickly cut	Juice of a lemon
Salt and black pepper	2 oz. butter, melted
½ teaspoon cayenne pepper	4 oz. lightly toasted breadcrumbs
½ teaspoon dry English mustard	Watercress or parsley for garnish

Season the lamb slices with salt and pepper, cayenne pepper and mustard. Place in a shallow dish and pour over the lemon juice. Cover and leave to marinate for 30 minutes. Set oven to 375°F or Mark 5. Remove the lamb slices from the marinade, brush with the melted butter and coat with breadcrumbs. Place in a greased roasting tin and bake for 15 minutes, or until completely heated through. Serve garnished with watercress or parsley and accompanied by creamed potatoes and grilled tomatoes. Serves 4.

Buckinghamshire Dumpling

A suet roly-poly containing bacon, liver and onions.

1 lb. prepared suet pastry	2 onions, peeled and finely
8 oz. streaky bacon rashers,	chopped
de-rinded	2 teaspoons chopped fresh
8 oz. pig's or lamb's liver,	parsley
wiped and sliced	1 teaspoon chopped sage
Pepper	

Roll out the pastry on a lightly floured surface to form a square about ¼-inch thick. Lay the bacon rashers on top, then cover with liver slices. Mix together the onion, herbs and pepper and sprinkle over. Dampen the edges, then roll up like a Swiss roll and press the ends together. Wrap up in a clean, well floured pudding cloth, then wrap again in kitchen foil. Tie the ends tightly, but allow the dumpling room to expand. Place in a saucepan of boiling water and boil for 2½–3 hours, topping up the water if necessary. Unwrap and serve cut into slices, accompanied by creamed potatoes and a rich brown gravy. Serves 4–6.

MILTON'S COTTAGE, CHALFONT ST. GILES

Braised Liver with Raisins and Almonds

A Buckinghamshire recipe.

2 oz. butter
2 small onions, peeled and sliced
1½ lb. lambs liver, wiped and
   cut into ½ inch slices
1 oz. plain flour

2 oz. seedless raisins or sultanas
1 teaspoon fresh chopped thyme
¼ pint red wine
1 pint lamb stock
Salt and black pepper

3 oz. blanched almonds, chopped

Melt 1 oz. butter in a frying pan and fry the onions until soft. Butter a shallow, ovenproof casserole dish. Dust the liver slices with flour and lay half of them in the casserole. Place the onions on top and sprinkle over half the raisins and all the thyme, then top with the remaining liver and raisins. Mix together the wine and stock and season. Pour over the liver. Cover and allow to stand for 10 minutes. Set oven to 350°F or Mark 4 and cook for 1–1¼ hours. Fry the almonds in the remaining 1 oz. of butter until golden. Remove the casserole from the oven and sprinkle over the almonds. Return to the oven and cook, uncovered, for 5 minutes. Serve with creamed potatoes, carrots and a green vegetable. Serves 4–6.

Oxford Marmalade

A dark chunky preserve, Oxford Marmalade at one time included ginger and black treacle.

3 lb. Seville oranges, wiped	6 pints water
1 small lemon, wiped	6 lb. preserving sugar

Peel the oranges and lemon and cut the peel into strips about 1–1½-inches long and ⅛-inch wide; this size can be adjusted to suite individual taste. Cut the flesh into small pieces and reserve the pips. Put the peel and the fruit into a large bowl and put the pips into a small one. Bring 6 pints of water to the boil. Pour 5 pints over the peel and fruit and the remaining pint over the pips. Cover both bowls and leave to stand overnight. Next day the pips will be covered in a soft jelly which has to be added to the peel and fruit. Lift the pips out of the water with a slotted spoon and place in a sieve set over a small bowl. Pour the pips' water over the pips into a bowl to wash off the jelly; repeat this procedure until the pips are clean. Discard the pips and pour the jelly water into the fruit water. Pour the peel, fruit and water into a preserving pan, bring to the boil and continue boiling until the peel is very soft – about 45–60 minutes. The longer the mixture boils the darker the finished marmalade will be. When the peel is soft, remove the preserving pan from the heat and add the sugar, stirring until it is dissolved. Bring slowly back to the boil and boil gently until the marmalade has become as dark as required. Then boil rapidly for 15 minutes. Test for 'set' and when setting point is reached, remove from the heat and skim the surface with a slotted spoon. Allow to stand for 15 minutes, then stir to distribute the peel evenly. Pour into clean, dry, warm jars, cover and label. Makes about 9 lb.

THE THAMES AT SHIPLAKE

Sweet Cake

An 18th century recipe that comes from Reading in Berkshire.

6 oz. butter, softened
4 oz. caster sugar
3 eggs and 2 egg yolks,
   beaten together

8 oz. plain flour
3 tablespoons brandy
3 tablespoons sherry
A little sifted icing sugar

Set oven to 350°F or Mark 4. Butter and line a 8-inch round cake tin. In a bowl, cream together the butter and sugar until light and fluffy, then beat in the beaten eggs. Add the flour a little at a time, beating well between each addition. Mix together the brandy and sherry and stir in, a little at a time, combining well. Turn the mixture into the prepared tin and bake for 1 hour, covering the top with a piece of kitchen foil if it appears to be browning too quickly. Cool in the tin for 5 minutes, then turn out on to a wire rack. Before serving, dust the top with a little sifted icing sugar.

Oxford Sausages

The recipe for these skinless sausages dates back to the 18th century.

1 lb. lean boneless pork
1 lb. lean boneless veal
12 oz. shredded suet
8 oz. fresh white breadcrumbs
Grated rind of half a lemon
1 teaspoon ground nutmeg

1 tablespoon chopped mixed
   fresh parsley, thyme, mint
   and marjoram
1 teaspoon chopped fresh sage
Salt and black pepper
1 egg, beaten

A little plain flour

Mince or *very* finely chop the pork and veal. Place in a large bowl and add the suet, breadcrumbs, lemon rind, nutmeg and all the herbs. Mix well together and season. Add the egg and stir well until the mixture is well combined and bound together. Flour the hands and form the mixture into sausage shapes. Dust lightly with flour and either cook the sausages under a hot grill, turning frequently until brown and cooked through, or fry in a mixture of oil and butter for about 8 minutes, turning frequently. Serve with creamed potatoes, grilled tomatoes and bacon. Makes approx. 24 sausages.

Berkshire Hog

The county of Berkshire is the home of the Black Berkshire breed of pig.

4 pork chops, wiped and
  trimmed
1 oz. butter
1 tablespoon oil
2 sprigs parsley, 1 sprig thyme,
  1 sage leaf and a bayleaf, tied
  together with a piece of string

½ pint white wine or pork stock
8 button onions, peeled
4 oz. mushrooms, wiped
  and sliced
1 tablespoon plain flour
¼ pint single cream
Salt and black pepper
Parsley sprigs for garnish

Heat the butter and oil together in a pan, then add the pork chops and brown lightly on both sides. Remove the chops, then add the onions and cook gently until golden. Add the wine or stock and *bouquet garni*, and return the chops to the pan. Bring to the boil, then cover and simmer gently for 45 minutes to 1 hour. Add the mushrooms and cook for a further 10 minutes. Blend the flour with a little of the cream. Remove the pan from the heat and stir in the flour mixture. Bring back to the boil and boil for 1 minute. Stir in the remainder of the cream and the seasoning and heat through, but do not allow to boil. Remove the herbs and serve, garnished with parsley sprigs and accompanied by creamed potatoes, carrots and a green vegtable. Serves 4.

Little Mutton Pies

A 19th century recipe, served at dinners given by the Duke of Buckingham.

¼ pint red wine
½ pint lamb stock
12 oz. lean lamb – ideally taken
  from the fillet end of a leg
  – finely chopped
1 onion, peeled and finely chopped

8 oz. mushrooms, wiped, trimmed
  and finely chopped
1 teaspoon chopped fresh thyme
1 teaspoon chopped fresh parsley
Salt and black pepper
1 lb. prepared puff pastry
1beaten egg for glazing

Boil the wine in a large saucepan until it is reduced by one-third, then stir in the stock. Add the lamb, onion, mushrooms, herbs and seasoning, bring to the boil then simmer for 30 minutes. Strain off

SONNING LOCK

the gravy and reserve and leave the meat mixture to get cold. Set oven to 375°F or Mark 5. Roll out the pastry on a lightly floured surface and use to line 8 small greased ramekin dishes, reserving approximately half the pastry for the lids. Divide the meat mixture evenly between the pies. Skim any fat from the top of the gravy and put 1 dessertspoonful into each pie. Place the lids on the pies, damping the edges and pressing them together. Crimp the edges to make a small ridge all round and make a small steam hole in the centre of each one. Brush well with beaten egg. Bake for 35–40 minutes or until the pastry is crisp and golden. Very carefully remove the pies from the dishes, and place on a wire rack. Heat the remaining gravy and pour a little into each pie through the steam hole in the top. Serve hot with creamed potatoes and a green vegetable, or cold with pickles.

THE CHURCHYARD CROSS, NORTH HINKSEY

Chiltern Hills Pudding

A steamed pudding containing dried fruit, suet and tapioca.

2 oz. tapioca	1 teaspoon bicarbonate of
¼ pint milk	soda dissolved in a little milk
1 tablespoon single cream	4 oz. fresh white breadcrumbs
4 oz. prepared suet	3 oz. sugar
4 oz. raisins or sultanas	A few drops of vanilla essence

In a bowl, soak the tapioca in the milk for 2 hours, then stir in the cream. Mix together the suet and the dried fruit. Add the bicarbonate of soda to the tapioca, then stir in the suet mixture, breadcrumbs, sugar and vanilla essence. Mix well together and turn into a well buttered 2–2½ pint pudding basin. Cover with a piece of greaseproof paper and a piece of kitchen foil and tie down. Place in a saucepan and add sufficient boiling water to come half way up the side of the basin and steam for 2½–3 hours, topping up the water as necessary. Turn out on to a warm serving dish and serve with cream, custard or vanilla sauce. Serves 4–6.

Spiced Oxford Cake

A dark cake containing raisins, peel, spice and treacle.

10 oz. plain flour	8 oz. raisins or sultanas
½ teaspoon baking powder	3 oz. chopped mixed peel
¾ teaspoon mixed spice	2 oz. black treacle, warmed slightly
6 oz. butter	Juice of half a lemon
6 oz. soft brown sugar	5 fl. oz. milk

Set oven to 350°F or Mark 4. Sift the flour, baking powder and spice together into a bowl and then rub in the butter until the mixture resembles fine breadcrumbs. Stir in the sugar, fruit and peel. Mix the treacle and lemon juice together and stir into the mixture, and then add sufficient milk to give a dropping consistency. Turn the mixture into a greased and base lined 8-inch round cake tin and bake for 1¾–2 hours, covering the top with a piece of kitchen foil if it appears to be browning too quickly. Allow to cool in the tin for 5 minutes, then turn out on to a wire rack.

Orange Tart

Queen Charlotte, wife of George III, was said to have been particularly fond of this dessert; the recipe comes from an 18th century Oxford manuscript.

8 oz. prepared shortcrust pastry	5 oz. caster sugar
Finely grated rind of 3 oranges	3 tablespoons cornflour
Grated rind and juice of 1 lemon	5 eggs, separated
Juice of 3 oranges made up to 14 fl. oz. with fresh orange juice	

Set oven to 400°F or Mark 6. Roll out the pastry on a lightly floured surface and use to line a greased 9-inch flan tin, trimming the edges neatly. Bake blind for 15–20 minutes. In a bowl mix together the orange and lemon rind, then add the orange juice and stir in 4 oz. of the sugar. Blend in the cornflour and pour the mixture into a saucepan. Bring to the boil, stirring, then reduce the heat and cook, still stirring, for 1 minute until smooth and thickened. Remove from the heat and stir in the lemon juice. Beat the egg yolks together and fold into the mixture. Pour into the flan case. Lower the oven temperature to 300°F or Mark 2. Whisk the egg whites with the remaining 1 oz. of sugar until they stand up in stiff peaks. Pile or pipe the egg whites on top of the filling, covering it completely, and bake for 30 minutes until the meringue is crisp and lightly golden. Serve hot or cold. Serves 4–6.

Lamb in Devil Sauce

Cold lamb simmered in a devil sauce. A light luncheon or supper dish from Buckinghamshire.

2 oz. butter	Salt and black pepper
1 small onion, peeled and very finely chopped	½ teaspoon cayenne pepper
2 tablespoons white wine vinegar	1 dessertspoon finely chopped fresh parsley
3 tablespoons redcurrant jelly	8 slices cold roast lamb
½ teaspoon French mustard	1 tablespoon tomato purée
Parsley sprigs for garnish	

Melt the butter in a frying pan and fry the onion until soft. Add the vinegar and redcurrant jelly and simmer, stirring, until the jelly has melted. Stir in the mustard, salt and pepper, cayenne pepper and parsley. Add the lamb slices and simmer gently for 5 minutes, or until the meat is fully heated through. If the sauce appears to be thickening too much, add 1–2 dessertspoons of stock. Remove the lamb from the sauce and arrange on a heated dish. Stir the tomato purée into the sauce and heat through thoroughly. Spoon over the lamb and serve garnished with parsley sprigs, and accompanied by boiled potatoes and green peas. Serves 4.

Aylesbury Roast Duck

Handsome white Aylesbury ducks were bred in Buckinghamshire, particularly around the town of Aylesbury. They are a delicious and popular table bird, traditionally served with orange sauce on Whit Sunday.

1 oven-prepared duck, about 5 lb.	**A little butter**
	Salt – ideally sea salt

ORANGE SAUCE

The rind and juice of 2 oranges	**2 tablespoons redcurrant jelly**
½ pint duck giblet stock	**2 tablespoons brandy**
4 tablespoons duck juices from the roasting tin	**Salt and black pepper**
1 tablespoon brown sugar	**1 orange, sliced, and a few watercress sprigs for garnish**

Set oven to 375°F or Mark 5. Prick the duck all over with a fork, then rub with butter and sprinkle with salt. Place in a roasting tin and roast, allowing about 20 minutes to the lb. plus an extra 15 minutes, and baste occasionally. Boil the duck neck and giblets with a small piece of celery, carrot and onion to make the stock. Remove the duck from the roasting tin, reserving the juices, and place on a hot serving dish. Keep warm. To make the Orange Sauce, place the rind and juice of the oranges in a saucepan. Strain the stock and add ½ pint to the oranges. Strain the duck juices and add about 4 tablespoons, together with the sugar, redcurrant jelly and brandy. Stir until the sugar and jelly are fully dissolved, then season and heat through thoroughly. Pour a little over the duck, garnish with orange slices and watercress sprigs and serve with roast potatoes and green peas and the remainder of the sauce. Serves 4.

Buckinghamshire Cherry Dumpers

Black Cherry orchards were once widespread in Buckinghamshire and on Cherry Pie Sunday, at the end of August when cherry picking was completed, these fruit turnovers were eaten. Traditionally they were accompanied by a tankard of ale.

1 lb. black cherries, pitted. If tinned cherries used, ensure that they are well drained

2 oz. granulated sugar
A little milk
Caster sugar

8 oz. prepared shortcrust pastry

Set oven to 400°F or Mark 6. Roll out the pastry on a lightly floured surface to about ⅛-inch thick, and cut out 4-inch circles. Divide the cherries evenly between these, piling them up on each circle, then sprinkle over the granulated sugar. Dampen the edges of the circles with a little cold water and fold up into turnovers, pinching the edges firmly together. Brush with milk and place on a lightly greased baking sheet. Bake for 20–30 minutes or until golden, then sprinkle with caster sugar while still hot. Serve hot or cold.

Ragout of Lamb

Ragouts, or rich stews, were popular from at least the 16th century – this Berkshire recipe dates from Regency times.

1 breast of lamb
2 oz. butter
1–1½ pints lamb stock
1 onion, peeled and left whole
15 cloves
3 carrots, peeled and finely sliced
4 oz. mushrooms, sliced
A walnut of butter

2 teaspoons lemon juice
4 sprigs parsley, 1 sprig thyme, 1 small sprig rosemary and a bayleaf tied together with a piece of kitchen string
Salt and black pepper
4 tablespoons cooked broad beans or green peas

Fresh chopped parsley for garnish

Cut the lamb into cubes, removing as much fat as possible, and dust with seasoned flour. Melt the butter and fry the lamb until golden. Heat the stock in a large saucepan. Stick the onion with the cloves, add to the stock and bring to the boil. Add the meat, cover, and simmer for 30 minutes. Lightly brown the carrots in the residual butter and add to the meat, together with the *bouquet garni* and simmer for 1½–2 hours, stirring from time to time. Lightly fry the mushrooms in the walnut of butter and lemon juice. Season and add to the meat together with the broad beans. Remove the herbs and the onion and cook for a further 10–15 minutes. Serve, garnished with chopped parsley and accompanied by creamed potatoes. Serves 4–6.

If desired, green peas cooked or frozen, can replace the broad beans, and the onion, with cloves removed, can be sliced and returned to the ragout just before serving.

AT OVING

Windsor Tartlets

A recipe from the 19th century, when figs were a popular dried fruit.

4 oz. plain flour
2 oz. butter, softened
1 egg yolk, beaten
2 oz. dried figs, very finely
  chopped
2 oz. ground almonds

2 oz. candied lemon peel,
  finely minced
1 teaspoon lemon juice
4 oz. apricot jam
1 egg, beaten
Additional apricot jam

A little caster sugar

Sift the flour into a bowl, then rub in the butter and bind the mixture with beaten egg yolk to form a soft dough. Chill for 15–20 minutes. Set oven to 375°F or Mark 5. Roll out the pastry thinly on a lightly floured surface and use to line 12–14 greased tartlet tins, trimming the edges neatly. Mix together the figs, ground almonds, lemon peel, lemon juice, jam and beaten egg, combining well. Place a little of the additional apricot jam in the base of each pastry case and divide the filling between them. Smooth over and sprinkle with a little caster sugar. Bake for 15–20 minutes until golden. Cool in the tins for 2 minutes, then place on a wire rack.

Beef Stew with Walnuts

A rich Berkshire stew.

1 lb. stewing steak
1 oz. dripping
1 onion, peeled and sliced
  or 8 button onions, peeled
2 fl. oz. red wine
1 pint beef stock
2 sprigs thyme and 4 sprigs
  parsley, tied together with
  a piece of kitchen string

Salt
Black pepper
12 button mushrooms, wiped
2 oz. chopped walnuts
1 stick of celery, trimmed and
  chopped
½ oz. butter
A little grated orange peel
  for garnish

Cut the steak into 2-inch cubes, dust with a little seasoned flour, and fry in the dripping until lightly browned. Remove with a slotted spoon and fry the onion in the residual dripping until golden.

Return the meat to the pan, and add the wine, stock, *bouquet garni* and seasoning. Bring to the boil, then cover and simmer for 1½–2 hours. Fry the mushrooms, walnuts and celery in the butter, and add to the stew after 1 hour of cooking. Remove the herbs and transfer the stew to a heated serving dish. Serve, garnished with grated orange peel and accompanied by creamed potatoes and a green vegetable. Serves 4.

Pancakes

Pancakes have been a popular dish since medieval days, but they are particularly associated with Shrove Tuesday, when they were a means of using up food, such as eggs, before the Lent fast began. The Buckinghamshire town of Olney is famous for its Shrove Tuesday Pancake Race, said to have its origins in the 14th century, when a housewife, frying pancakes, heard the church bell ring and, not wanting to be late for the service, ran to church, frying pan in hand and still wearing her apron.

3 oz. plain flour	½ pint milk
Pinch of salt	1–2 oz. melted butter
3 eggs	Lemon juice and caster sugar
Lemon slices for decoration	

Sift the flour and salt together into a bowl. Make a well in the centre and add the eggs, beating well. Then gradually stir in the milk, beating until a smooth, creamy batter is formed. Leave the batter to stand in a cool place for 10–15 minutes. Grease an omelette or frying pan with butter and heat until smoking hot. Stir the melted butter into the batter, and spoon in enough batter to coat the pan lightly. Cook for about ½-minute until lightly set on top and golden underneath, then toss, or turn with a palette knife, to cook the topside. Cooking only takes about 1 minute. Sprinkle the pancake with lemon juice and sugar, roll up or fold into a triangle, and serve immediately from the pan, decorated with a slice of lemon. Make the remainder of the pancakes in the same way, serving them piping hot. Serves 4.

Although lemon and sugar are traditional, warm apricot jam 'spiked' with a little lemon juice, makes a delicious alternative.

BABLOCKHYTHE FERRY, RIVER THAMES

Buckingham Cakes

Small sponge cakes flavoured with ginger.

2 eggs	½ teaspoon baking powder
4 oz. butter	1 teaspoon ground ginger
4 oz. caster sugar	1½ oz. preserved ginger,
4 oz. plain flour	finely chopped
A little sifted icing sugar	

Set oven to 375°F or Mark 5. Beat the eggs in a bowl set over a pan of warm water until fluffy. Cream the butter and sugar together until light and fluffy, then gradually beat in the eggs. Sift together the flour, baking powder and ground ginger and fold into the mixture, then fold in the preserved ginger. Spoon the mixture into buttered and floured patty tins and bake for 15 minutes, until golden and springy to the touch. Cool on a wire rack. Before serving, dust with sifted icing sugar. Makes between 12 and 16 cakes.

Duke of Windsor's Gingerbread

This gingerbread was reputed to have been a favourite with the Duke of Windsor, later Edward VIII, when he was a child.

8 oz. plain flour	1 oz. mixed candied peel,
4 oz. butter	chopped
4 oz. soft brown sugar	8 oz. black treacle, warmed
½ oz. ground ginger	¼ teaspoon bicarbonate of
½ teaspoon ground allspice	soda
4 oz. almonds, blanched	1 egg
and chopped	2 tablespoons milk

Set oven to 350°F or Mark 4. Sift the flour into a bowl, then rub in the butter until the mixture resembles fine breadcrumbs. Stir in the sugar, spices, almonds and peel. Mix the treacle and bicarbonate of soda together and beat into the mixture. Beat the egg and milk together and stir into the mixture, combining well. Pour into a greased and floured 2 lb. loaf tin and bake for 40 minutes. Cool in the tin for 5 minutes, then turn out on to a wire rack. Serve sliced and spread with butter.

Rout Cakes

Like Rout Biscuits, and also from Middlesex, these cakes were eaten at fashionable gatherings or routs.

8 oz. plain flour	1 oz. currants
½–¾ oz. butter	2 fl. oz. brandy
2 oz. caster sugar	A few drops orange flower
2 oz. candied orange and	water
lemon peel, mixed	2 small eggs, beaten
A little sifted icing sugar	

Set oven to 425°F or Mark 7. Sift the flour into a bowl, then rub in the butter. Stir in the sugar, peel and currants, and then add the brandy and orange flower water. Mix to a soft, dropping consistency with sufficient of the beaten egg (all of it may not be required) and place teaspoons of the mixture, set well apart, on a greased baking sheet. Bake for 10 minutes until golden. Cool on a wire rack and dust lightly with sifted icing sugar before serving.

Buckinghamshire Rabbit Pie

A puff pastry pie with rabbit, cheese, macaroni and double cream.

A 2–2½ lb. rabbit, jointed	1 small onion, peeled and
2 sprigs thyme, 4 sprigs parsley,	finely chopped
a sage leaf and a bayleaf,	2 oz. Cheddar cheese, grated
tied together with a	2 teaspoons chopped fresh
piece of kitchen string	parsley
1 onion peeled and stuck	1 teaspoon chopped fresh thyme
with 6 cloves	½ pint double cream
Salt and black pepper	8 oz. prepared puff pastry
2 oz. short cut macaroni	A little beaten egg

Soak the rabbit joints in cold salted water for 1½ hours. Drain well. Place in a saucepan, cover with fresh water and bring to the boil. Skim, then add the *bouquet garni*, the onion stuck with cloves and seasoning. Cover and simmer for 1–1½ hours, until the rabbit is tender. Remove the rabbit and strain and reserve the stock. Allow the rabbit to cool slightly, then remove the meat from the bones.

Bring the reserved stock to the boil and add the macaroni. Boil until tender, then drain the macaroni and mix with the rabbit meat. Stir in the onion, grated cheese and herbs and season. Turn the rabbit mixture into a 2-pint pie dish and place a pie funnel in the centre. Pour over the cream. Set oven to 425°F or Mark 7. Roll out the pastry on a lightly floured surface and cut off a narrow band. Dampen the rim of the pie dish with cold water and press the pastry band on to it, trimming the edges neatly. Brush with cold water and top with a lid from the remaining pastry, trimming the edges neatly and pressing the edges down well with a fork. Cut two small slits in the pastry lid as steam vents, then brush with beaten egg. Bake for 40 minutes or until golden brown. Serve with creamed potatoes and carrots. Serves 4–6.

AN OLD CORNER, IVINGHOE

METRIC CONVERSIONS

The weights, measurements and oven temperatures used in the
preceding recipes can be easily converted to their metric equivalents.

Weights

Avoirdupois	Metric
1 oz.	just under 30 grams
4 oz. (¼ lb.)	app. 115 grams
8 oz. (½ lb.)	app. 230 grams
1 lb.	454 grams

Liquid Measures

Imperial	Metric
1 tablespoon (liquid only)	20 millilitres
1 fl. oz.	app. 30 millilitres
1 gill (¼ pt.)	app. 145 millilitres
½ pt.	app. 285 millilitres
1 pt.	app. 570 millilitres
1 qt.	app. 1.140 litres

Oven Temperatures

	°Fahrenheit	Gas Mark	°Celsius
Slow	300	2	140
	325	3	158
Moderate	350	4	177
	375	5	190
	400	6	204
Hot	425	7	214
	450	8	232
	500	9	260

KENNET AND AVON CANAL AT NEWBURY